"Hi. I'm Ann. I'm an ordinary girl who is out to change my world."

Ann Kiemel, a former high school teacher and youth director in a large church on the West Coast, is currently dean of women at Eastern Nazarene College in Massachusetts.

She is in great demand across the country as a speaker at conferences and youth retreats.

Almost every weekend she travels somewhere to share her inspiring faith with others of all ages, in all walks of life. She has seen the difference faith can make. This is her story. It's about Ann and the people she meets.

"Ann takes the ordinary happenings of her days and, with an engaging poetic style, lets us experience with her the power of God in Christ reconciling the world to himself—one life at a time."   —Charles Colson

I'm Out
to Change
My World

Ann Kiemel

A KANGAROO BOOK
PUBLISHED BY POCKET BOOKS NEW YORK

dedicated to jan, my sister . . .
she makes me believe in love

I'M OUT TO CHANGE MY WORLD

Impact Books edition published 1974

POCKET BOOK edition published July, 1977

This POCKET BOOK edition includes every word contained in
the original, higher-priced edition. It is printed from brand-
new plates made from completely reset, clear, easy-to-read type.
POCKET BOOK editions are published by
POCKET BOOKS,
a Simon & Schuster Division of
GULF & WESTERN CORPORATION
1230 Avenue of the Americas,
New York, N.Y. 10020.
Trademarks registered in the United States
and other countries.

ISBN: 0-671-81043-0.
Library of Congress Catalog Card Number: 74-81137.
This POCKET BOOK edition is published by arrangement
with Impact Books, a division of John T. Benson Publishing
Company. Copyright, ©, 1974, by Impact Books, a division
of John T. Benson Publishing Company. All rights reserved.
This book, or portions thereof, may not be reproduced by
any means without permission of the original publisher:
Impact Books, a division of John T. Benson Publishing
Company, 1625 Broadway, Nashville, Tennessee 37202.

Printed in the U.S.A.

ACKNOWLEDGMENTS

Our thanks to the following publishers for permission to quote from the following copyrighted songs:

"God Can Do Anything." Copyright, 1946, by Singspiration. All rights reserved. Used by permission. Composed by Ira Stanphill.

"I Will Serve Thee." Copyright, ©, 1969, by William J. Gaither. International copyright secured. All rights reserved. Used by permission. Composed by Bill and Gloria Gaither.

"Lonely Voices." Copyright, ©, 1967, by Hope Publishing Company. International copyright secured. All rights reserved. Used by permission. Composed by Billie Hanks, Jr.

"Something Beautiful." Copyright, ©, 1971, by William J. Gaither. International copyright secured. All rights reserved. Used by permission. Composed by Bill and Gloria Gaither.

"Without Him." Copyright, ©, 1963, by The LeFevres. International copyright secured. All rights reserved. Used by permission. Composed by Mylon LeFevre.

Contents

Introduction

"Finally brethren, whatever is true, whatever is
honorable, whatever is just, whatever is pure,
whatever is lovely, whatever is gracious, if there
is any excellence, if there is anything worthy of
praise, think about these things. What you have
learned and received and heard and seen in me,
do; and the God of peace will be with you."

When Paul wrote to the Phillipians he might have
had Ann Kiemel in mind. To be with Ann is to see
Paul's thoughts come alive before your eyes. Whenever
our paths have crossed, however briefly, I have always
come away infused with the quiet joy from her child-
like faith, her special ability to see the world through
the eyes of our Lord Jesus Christ.

In I'M OUT TO CHANGE MY WORLD, Ann
takes the ordinary happenings of her days and, with
an engaging poetic style, lets us experience with her
the power of God in Christ reconciling the world to
Himself—one life at a time.

Ann Kiemel's life and writings are proof of the truth
that God uses ordinary people and ordinary happenings to launch the work of His saints—and change
His world. St. Augustine hears the voice of a small

child; an anonymous Moravian reads Luther to John Wesley; a shoe clerk named Dwight Moody, while wrapping shoes, listens to a dry goods salesman talk about Christ; the great Dutch theologian and political leader Abraham Kuyper was converted by a peasant woman who after listening to one of Kuyper's sermons told him that he must be born again; Charles Haddon Spurgeon seeks refuge from a snowstorm in a church while a workingman in the pulpit talks about Jesus. In each instance, a seemingly insignificant person—or encounter—was the turning point in the life of these great servants of God.

Who is to say who is great in God's eyes? "For the wisdom of this world is foolishness before God." Ann Kiemel's story is another chapter in the great unfolding drama of how God, not man, chooses His people. What a blessing it is to read in these pages the beautifully told story of how God is using one woman's life.

Charles W. Colson
Washington, D.C.
February 3, 1977

THE AGNOSTIC

I whipped into a small gas station,
"Uhm, sir,
        could you fill it up please?
            I'm kind of in a big hurry.
                I'm on my way to the airport."
                                "Oh, you are, are you?
                                Where are you going, lady?"
"Oklahoma City."
                        "Going to visit friends there?"
"No, sir, I'm going to speak."
                            "What do *you* speak about?"
And I stuck my head out of the car window
        and I said,
    "Hi, sir. My name is Ann.
        Did you really want to know?"
                                "Yeah, that's why I asked."
"Well you see, sir,

12

Jesus Christ is the Lord of my life.
        He laughs with me
             and cries with me
                and . . ."
                             "I'm an agnostic, ma'am."
"Wow! An AGNOSTIC?
    A real AGNOSTIC?
        I don't meet many of those.
    Uhm, tell me sir,
        do you have any problems?"
                    "Yeah, I've got a lot of them."
"Tell me one."
                He squatted down beside my window
                  and looked in as he said,
                      "I'm so insignificant."
                He face was sober
                  and his voice was so bitter
                    as he said,
                      "I'm so insignificant."
"Sir, me too.
I'm just an ordinary girl
    but Jesus adds a lot to my life."
        And I began sharing Christ with the attendant
    'til the gas started spilling out over the car
                  and he ran
                  and grabbed the pump
                  and washed off the car
                  and . . .
"Sir, I'm really going to have to go.
    I'm afraid I might miss my plane."

13

Suddenly, I saw this dirty, grimy hand
reaching through the window.
I didn't care if it was dirty—
"Brother,
I'll take your hand.
I'll walk with you
in the name of Christ
I'll love you to Jesus."
He looked through the window at me—
"You know lady,
for the first time in my life
you've made me want to believe.
Thank you."
I'm going where He goes . . .
Will you?
And He'll be there beside me.
The love for which He died
Is all I need to guide me.
And He's my gold . . .
Is He yours?
And my silver brightly shining . . .
He writes the music
on a quiet summer morning.

I'm an ordinary girl in a big world
but I'm going to change it—
God and I
and love.
"Yes sir, I'll walk with you.
And you, ma'am.

14

And you."
You and I together,
we can make it.
Believe with me in the world where you live.
I need you,
and God needs you.

GOD IS SO GOOD

I was flying to Florida just recently
and I was seated next to a surgeon.

"Sir?
You know what, sir?
I know you would find this hard to believe
but do you know what I did at 5:00 A.M.
this morning?
I just happened to awaken out of a dark sleep,
and sir, I just lay in bed and cried.
Because you see, sir,
I am a Christian
and Jesus is the Lord of my life.
And sir,
I'm so glad that He walks with me
and that He even chose to invade my life
and live in my humble apartment
and laugh with me

18

and cry with me
and understand me.
Sir,
do you know what I did at 5:00 this morning?
I just slipped out of my bed
on my knees
just to weep out my love for Him.

"I love Him, sir.
He is more than just a great God high above,
He's the Lord of my life.
He puts His hand on my shoulder
and He wipes my tears.
I hear Him laughing when I laugh,
I feel His silence when I am silent."

The surgeon turned and shook his head and said
    "Young lady,
        some people might laugh at you,
            but I'd like to have that kind of faith in God,
            How did you find it?"

            "C. S. Lewis says,
    'Either we say Jesus Christ is a great man,
        or we fall on our faces and say,
            He is the Lord.'
    I have problems,
    as a matter of fact,
    in my own private world
    in a way I can't share.

19

I am walking the loneliest road I've ever
walked,
I didn't know a desert could be so dry
but I love Him,
I really love Him.
And I know a simple girl named Ann doesn't
walk alone,
a great big Lord has chosen to invade her life
and walk with her.
He is so good."

God is so good.
God is so good, God is so good.
He's so good to me.

If you have eyes to see
or a little boy next to you
or if you have someone to call a friend
if you felt the warm sunlight in your face today
or saw the blue sky and laughed
you must know what it means to sing
'God is so good.'
If you know what it feels like to laugh with God,
to have fallen flat on your face
and have Him reach out
and say I still love you, take my hand;
to feel Him lift your guilt,
to ease your pain,
to have Him soothe your tired,
worn, broken heart,

then you must understand how good He is.
So sing with me,

**God is so good.
God is so good, God is so good.
He's so good to me.
I love Him so,
I love Him so, I love Him so.
He's so good to me."**

TAXI DRIVER

It was in the summer
        and I got into a beat up old cab in Miami Beach
            and asked the old cab driver
        to take me to another hotel.
        It was hot
            and every window was rolled down.

And I asked him,
"What is the one word
    that describes your life?"
                            "Can I give you two?"
                                        he said.

He was old and gnarled,
        about as beat up as his cab.
"Yes," I said.
    "What are they?"
                        "Bored
                            and unhappy."

24

"Sir,
   why are those the two words
that describe your life?"

                    "I don't know.
                           I guess 'cause
                    I got nobody in the world."
"Nobody, Sir?
   No wife, no children, no family?
No one in the whole world for you?"
                           "No."
"Tell me, Sir,
   how did you get to be an old man
and have nobody?"

                    " 'Cause I never got a good job
                           and no woman wanted me."
"Sir,
   can I sing you a song?"
                           "Sing?"
"I don't have a very good voice,
   but I know you'd like my song."
                    "Just a minute, please."
                    He rolled up his window.
                    Then he nodded at me.

And I began to sing:

              Something beautiful,
              something good.
              All my confusion
              He understood.

                    25

All I had to offer Him
was brokenness and strife.
But He's making something beautiful
out of my life.

"Sir,
   do you know who I'm singing about?
Jesus Christ, He's the Lord of my life.
   He laughs with me
and cries with me—"
                                        "I'm a Jew."
"Sir, He'll walk with you.
   He'll laugh with you.
He'll be your friend."

And just then we pulled under the portico of the next
         hotel
         and I was fumbling in my purse for my money
             when I saw this old hand reach out
                 and I let loose of the money in my purse.
   I reached out and took his hand
         almost afraid to look him in the eye
         because I didn't know what he would say.
   I lifted my eyes to his
         and he was crying.
                        "Lady,
               when I got in this old cab tonight
   I was the loneliest person in the whole world.
   I never heard anyone talk like you talked tonight
               and I want your God.

26

He and I could ride together."

And I crawled out of that old cab
  knowing that somewhere in Miami Beach
    an old, gnarled, wrinkled man
  drives a beat up old cab.
    But he doesn't drive alone.
  And I can hardly help but sing
    when I know that the eternal God
  is willing to invade an old cabbie's life
    and love him.

HOMESICK G.I.

I boarded a plane in San Antonio
  and I had been speaking to 500 teen-agers that week
    and I was exhausted.   ..
I asked the stewardess,
    "Would you mind if I had a seat by myself,
      I'm just so exhausted."
She said she understood
    and she put me by a window
      with the whole row cleared of everybody else.
I looked out the window,
  I was going home,
    and I love to go home.
I was going home knowing that 500 teen-agers in
      Texas
    believed with me for my world.
          And the sky was yellow and orange
            and the sun was setting.

I knew there were other people on board
    but I just started to sing:

                        This is my story
                        this is my song.
                  I really felt like singing.
                  Praising my Saviour
                  All the day long.
                  Oh Jesus,
                  I want to sing about you.
                  I want people to hear me
                        sing about you.
                  This is my story
                  this is my song.
                  Praising my Saviour
                  All the day long.

And out of the clear blue sky
    I heard a man's voice say,
"Uh, ma'am,
    do you hate to leave San Antonio?"
                And I turned around
                      and there was a young kid
                      and I wondered where he came from.
    "Uh-uh,
                I don't mind at all.
            Do you sir?"
"Yes, ma'am, I do."
                His face got sober.
"You see, I just got back from Viet Nam
    about two weeks ago
and I saw two of my best buddies

31

murdered before my very eyes.
And then when I got home
    my wife was gone
and all the family I have left
    is right here in Texas
and I'm going back to war."
                    "I'm sorry, sir.
                        I didn't know your world
                    was so ugly."
"Lady,
    was that you singing
a minute ago?"
                    "Yeah, it was."
"Lady,
    what makes you so happy?"

And I turned and looked him in the eye.
                "Sir, my name is Ann.
                    Do you really want to know?
                You see, I'm a Christian
                    and Jesus is the Lord of my life.
                He laughs with me
                    and cries with me
                and walks lonely roads with me.
                    And, sir,
                He and I are out to change the world.
                    And, sir,
                He can change your world."
The tears began flowing
    down that young G.I.'s face.

32

And he looked at me.
"I never knew a God like you have
     How do you find Him?"

And I opened my purse
     and pulled a card out
          and wrote a prayer on it.
     Not a special prayer,
               a prayer off my head,
                    I just wrote it on a card
               and handed it to him.
                    "Sir, if you'll pray this prayer
                         and mean it,
                    Jesus will become your friend
                         and Lord of your life."
And that's all that was said the entire flight
     and I had taken a nap
          and the plane was on its descent.
Suddenly, he leaned over to me and said,
"Ann, excuse me,
     I know you're tired and everything
but I wanted to tell you something.
     I wanted to thank you.
I prayed that prayer
     and I don't feel alone anymore.
And Ann, I think God and I—
     we can make it."
                    And I reached out and took his hand.
                    "Sir, you and God,
                         you can make it.

Anywhere and through anything.
Remember this:
God and I,
we're walking with you."

And I deboarded that plane
and there were thousands of people in the airport
but I really believed,
that I had the most important mission
of any of the people hurrying about me
because I had changed my world
in just a little way.

I'd reminded a broken, lonely G.I.
that Jesus lived and loved
and would walk with him.

Lonely eyes.
I see them in the subway.
I do—we have subways in Boston you know.
People burdened by the troubles of the day.
Men at leisure
but they are so unhappy,
Tired of foolish games they try to play
Lonely voices fill my dreams.
Do they yours, Sir?
Your voice sounds lonely, your face looks empty.
Sir, take my hand. I'll walk with you.
I'll be your friend.

34

ORDINARY DAYS

> **Something beautiful**
> **something good**
> **All my confusion, He understood**
> **All I had to offer Him,**
> **was brokenness and strife**
> **But He's making something beautiful**
> **out of my life.**

Sometimes people say,
  "Ann, I want to speak like you.
    I want to do like you.
      I want to be a dean of women at a college.
    What do I do to be like you?"
And I look back over my life
    and I remember being that little girl
      with my father on long walks
    and him saying to me,
      "Remember just this . . .
        It pays.

It pays to serve Jesus."
I grew up in Hawaii
    and don't tell me what prejudice is.
        I know.
I was one light face in the middle
    of several thousand dark faces on my campus.
I cannot remember one night in my junior high years
    that I did not cry myself to sleep
        and wonder why my face couldn't be dark, too.
    I wondered why Hindus and Buddhists
        had to laugh at my God.
    I wondered why friends laughed behind my back
        because I was a foreigner.
And all through my junior high years,
        I kept saying,
            "Daddy, why does it pay to serve Jesus?"
                And my father would say,
                    "Hang in there.
                        It pays."
            And so many mornings, I'd say,
                "Mom, I don't want to go to school today."
And she'd push me out the door
        with my brother and sister and say,
"Don't you kids know
        that life is made up of ordinary days
            when there's no one to pat you on the back?
        When there's no one to praise you?
            When there's no one to honor you?
        When there's no one to see how brave and noble
            you are?

Almost all of life is made up of ordinary days.
    And it's how you live your ordinary days
        that determines whether or not you have big
        moments.
    Get out there
        and make something of your ordinary days."
And I'd stumble out the door in tears.
And I still remember the last day in my large high
    school.
My sister and I were on the platform to receive little
    awards
        but a lot of kids could make A's.
    And we were getting scholarships
        but whoever heard of Northwest Nazarene
        College?
And when they would make the announcements,
    the students would give slight applause
        and they would go on.
    And then the principal called Jan and me.
        He said,
            "We're Hindus and Buddhists,
                but these two girls came
            and brought their God to our campus.
            They've changed our world."
        And I can only remember the applause
            and that it never seemed to end.
    I was speechless.
        I can remember the tears dripping off my chin.
Inside I was whispering
"Daddy you were right.

Through the thousands of ordinary days
  when I wanted to give up, it paid.
It pays to be true.
  It pays to follow Jesus."

And I went to college
  and faced good days and ordinary days.
But when I was a junior,
   it came to me.
    "Ann, either you are going to follow
     Jesus Christ to the end
    or not follow Him at all."
After all,
  I was an honor student.
  I was becoming somebody on campus.
   I had big dreams.
    I had high hopes.
Follow Jesus to the end?
  What if I never had a dream come true?
   What if nothing special ever happened?
  Nothing I ever loved ever came my way?
   Would I follow Jesus to the end,
  if everything I loved was taken away?
Would I make that kind of decision to follow?
For you it might have been an easy decision.
  For me it was six long months—
     ugly months—
      of struggle.
    "Jesus, how can I?"
  'Til I remember kneeling by the couch

in the TV room
    and piling into my hands all that I loved
and knowing what it meant for the first time,
"Yes, Lord, from now to the end I will follow
    you."
        Yes, Lord
        to anything
        anytime, anywhere.
        Yes, Lord—if you'll go with me.
That was really the turning point in my life.
    I chose on my own
        to follow Jesus to the end.
    I don't know what it will mean to follow to
        the end.
        I have a feeling it's a long road,
            and there are a lot of mountains.
But I love nothing better than adventure,
        and I'm ready to climb.

SPINACH AND DREAMS

I was a sophomore in college
　　and my sister and I had to work our way through
　　and someone suggested we work at Birdseye.
　　The pay was terrific, they said,
　　　and with the other scholarships and all,
　　　　if you could get on at Birdseye
　　you could pay your way through college.
And Jan and I said,
　　If they'll just call us,
　　　　we can make thousands of dollars.
　　They said, of course,
　　　　that the turnover among girls was high,
　　　　　　most girls last one night.
　　But Jan and I said,
　　　　"We're tough,
　　　　　　we can make it."

And when the foreman called and said we had the job,
　　we thought it was the biggest event in history.

We had heard stories about my Dad—
>   how he worked his way through school.
We were going to do the same.
Every night—
>   from 6:00 P.M. to 6:00 A.M.

The first night
>   we put on our freshly starched white jeans and
>   sweatshirts, fixed our hair just perfect
>   and headed to work.
>   We could hardly wait—
> $1.65 an hour!
The first thing they did
>   was put a hairnet on us that ruined our hairdo
>   and had a big bill on it that said BIRDSEYE.
The second thing they did to us
>   was stand us by a moving belt
>   of cold, wet, spinach.
>   *I like nearly every vegetable in the*
>   *world,*
>   *but spinach, I can't stand.*
and the supervisor said we were to sort out the
>   bad spinach
>   and leave the good spinach on the belt—
>   all night.
>   That was our job.

By midnight
>   I didn't know which was good spinach and which
>   was bad

and I was too scared to ask
and hated it all.
So I pulled spinach
as if I really knew what I was doing.
and I was sick of spinach juice in my face.
The machinery was so loud
I didn't think I could stand it another minute
and we had six hours to go.
I was shivering from the cold
and I began to sing
every hymn I could think of
that had the word "victory" in it.
No one could hear me it was so noisy.
I sang may way through the night.
At 6:00 A.M. the next morning,
my jeans were green
my sweatshirt was green
and I had spinach juice on my face.
And my sister and I stumbled home
and into my parents' room
and fell across their bed sobbing,
"Daddy, I don't care if I never have another pair of
shoes.
I don't care about another new dress.
I don't want a college education.
Daddy, you won't make us go back, will you?"
All our parents could do was laugh—
we looked so pathetic.
My father said,
"Go to bed.

44

You'll feel better when you wake up."
I felt lousy when I woke up.
        But I did go back to BIRDSEYE.
            My sister went back east to school
but I worked the whole summer.

On the last night of the summer crew
    the foreman of the crew came up to me.
"Ann, you're our longest term female employee."
                        "Really," I said.
"Yeah.
    You must really be poor."
                    "Sir, you're right.
                        I'm very poor.
            "But that's not why I stayed on this job.
    I'd rather be poor.
But God and I have big dreams, sir.
        And with big dreams you have to keep on,
if you give up in one little area,
        the next big thing that comes up
you'll want to give up in that, too.
        And with big dreams, sir,
            you just can't give up."

THREE ROWS EVERY SUNDAY

So I went to teach school in Kansas City
　　　and never forgot that lesson.
You know where I lived in Kansas City?
　　　One room, upstairs, no heat,
　　　　　　no air conditioning,
　　　　　　　　　a bed that sagged
　　　　　　and a lamp stand.
　　　I was teaching school every day
　　　　　　and every night I would awaken
　　　　　　　　suddenly.
　　　　　　"Jesus, I'm scared.
　　That sophisticated-pseudo-sophisticated campus
　　with those pseudo-sophisticated teachers,
　　　and the anti-religious principal.
　　　　　How can I share You with them?"

Those were the loneliest days of my life,
　　　but I remember one day when I scooted my chair
　　　　　　back,

it was between classes,
       and went out in the hall
and I began to grab kids.
"Do you go to church anywhere?
    I've got something exciting to tell you.
    Would you come to church with me?"
The first Sunday my little Ghia was packed.
    The next Sunday it was, too.
        On the next Sunday I asked my church for a
           bus.
And I began to fill it with students.
        On Sunday morning it wasn't an unusual
           sight
           to see me coming down the aisles with 25
              kids,
        the drop-outs,
           the most popular.
And we'd fill up three rows every Sunday.

And every Sunday morning
    some little old lady would come up to me and say,
"Honey, have you talked to the principal about this?"
            "Well, no, I haven't.
                It's only on Sundays,
                and I haven't really said anything."
But one morning I said,
    "This is the reckoning.
I know I'm going to be persecuted like Paul.
    This is the end of my job,
        but I've got to tell him."

And I walked into the principal's office.
I was scared to death of Mr. Wallace.
"Sir, you gave me accelerated students
        and I've crammed knowledge into their brains,
but it takes more than that to make a person.
        I believe that because I'm a Christian, sir,
                and I also believe that without Christ
                        there is no meaning to life,
        and so, sir,
        I need to tell you that every Sunday morning
                I've been bringing a bus to school and
                        picking up students and taking them
                                to church with me.
        I'm out to change my world
                and I don't know where else to begin.
        He looked up and a smile spread across his face.
"You know,
you can't believe how many phone calls we've gotten.
        Parents who can't do a thing with their kids
                think it's the greatest thing that ever happened.
        I never knew a teacher who could spend five days
                with kids
        and want to spend a sixth with them.
                But if you want to, it's okay with me."
I stumbled out the door
        with a sense of shock and surprise and excitement.
                **I'm going where He goes
                and He'll be there to guide me.
                His love is all I need
                        to guide me.**

No, not the perfect words,
not the very right situations,
not the very right opportunities,
And He's my gold,
And my silver brightly shining
He writes the music on quiet summer mornings.

Every afternoon
I would park in front of the Milican High School
        campus.
    It was the biggest campus in Long Beach.
And every afternoon I would park there
    when the kids got out of school
    and I would just watch them.
And every afternoon I would whisper,
      "Oh, Jesus,
I don't know how I can get on this campus
    but Jesus, it's part of my world."
  And the kids looked so aimless
      and so empty
      and so lonely
      and I wanted to share my Christ with them.
One afternoon
I remember literally

putting my arms up around the steering wheel
and burying my face and sobbing.
It seemed so hopeless.
The policies for any kind of a Christian touch
on a campus in Southern California
are so strict.
And I didn't think
that there would be any way
that I actually could get on the Milican
campus—and help change it.
But it suddenly came to me one day—
why didn't I go to the principal?
I mean he was the head of the school
and he had the say about everything—
why didn't I confront him?
Well, I didn't know a thing
about Milican's high school principal
but I called the secretary and asked her
if I could see him.
"Well, you know he's a very busy
man
and I really don't think he can take an appointment,
but I'll check with him."
She came back to the telephone and
said,

"Well,
he says he'll see you this afternoon.
How will that be?"
And I said,
"Just great."

55

I didn't know what I would say to him
but I walked into his office and said,
"Hi, Mr. Woods.
My name is Ann.
I live in your world—
Everyday I drive by your campus
and I look at your students.
You see, Mr. Woods,
I'm a Christian.
Jesus Christ is the Lord of my life—
He laughs with me
and cries with me
and walks lonely roads with me.
Oh, Mr. Woods,
I've been a teacher with accelerated students
and I know
it takes more than cramming knowledge into kids'
brains to make their lives fulfilled.
Mr. Woods,
I know this sounds ridiculous.
I know what your policies are on this campus.
I know you haven't even allowed
Campus Life
or Youth for Christ
to come to campus.
But Mr. Woods,
I will sweep floors,
I will clean rooms,
I'll do secretarial work—
I'll do anything you have for me to do

56

if you'll just give me a chance
to live
and breathe
and share
with the students on your campus."
I couldn't believe it
when he looked up and said,
"Well, Miss Kiemel, you're very convincing.
You know, I've never heard anyone
with that kind of positive approach before.
As a matter of fact,
I do have an idea.
Once in a while,
if I'm really impressed,
I'll offer a forum on campus.
You could come on campus
and hold a forum for the students.
I know how busy you must be
and I can get the print shop
to make up all the posters
and do all the advertising.
How would that be?

I stammered out that that would be wonderful
and walked out of his office
with a sense of awe
and simple joy
because of a giant of a God inside me
and because I, an ordinary girl,
am linked to an extraordinary God

and there is nothing that is impossible.

That night
　　　the student president of Milican High School
　　　　　called,
"Is this Ann Kiemel?
Ann Kiemel, who are you?
Are you some kind of angel or something?
I'm Mike so-and-so,
　　　the student body president at Milican.
　　　Do you know Mr. Woods, our principal?"
　　　　　　　　　　　　　　"Well," I said,
　　　　　　　　　　　　"I met him this afternoon."
"Are you trying to tell me
that Mr. Woods is allowing you on campus
to hold a Christian forum?
I don't believe it.
I can hardly get in to see him.

　　　　　He allows nothing with the word 'Christian'
　　　　　　　stamped on it
　　　　　　　　at anytime
　　　　　　　　or anywhere
　　　　　　　　　on his campus."
　　　　　　　　"Well, I don't understand it.
　　　　　　　　But all I know
　　　　　　　　is that he told me
　　　　　　　　I could do it.
　　　　　　　　He even volunteered
　　　　　　　　to have all the publicity
　　　　　　　　done for me."

"Would you come over to the campus tomorrow?
I want to meet you.
I really do believe you are an angel."

The next afternoon I met the student body president
    and I shared my Christ with him
        and my hope for the world.

I brought all my teenagers together and said,
    "Mr. Woods has given us this opportunity,
        what shall be our theme?"
            And we prayed,
            and we dreamed,
            and we thought—
    what would be our theme?
                Finally one of the kids asked,
    "Why don't we just plaster ANN all over campus
        and create such a spirit of inquisitiveness
        that they come to find out who ANN is?"
Well, it scared me
    but it did seem to be kind of a good idea.
        I mean it was unique and original.
                So I called Mr. Woods
            and he agreed
            and the print shop went to work.

I have never been more scared—
            before or since in my life
        as I was that afternoon
            on the way to Milican High.

It was the roughest campus in Long Beach—
    would they walk out on me,
    would they boo,
    would they throw tomatoes?
                I didn't know.
                Nervously,
            I walked on campus
        and mingled with the students
    who had just gotten out of class.
      They looked hard and indifferent.
When I walked into the huge auditorium
    I couldn't believe it was nearly packed.
      The student body president
           asked if he could introduce me
           and he did.

I started just like I always do.
                "Hi, I'm Ann.
            I'm a nobody.
            I live in a big world.
            But I'm out to change it.
            You see, I'm a Christian.
            I believe in Jesus Christ.
              He's the Lord of my life.
He laughs with me
    and cries with me
        and walks lonely roads with me.
      And He'll walk with you."
        And I began to share with them
        how they could find Jesus Christ

and how he could become their Lord.
I couldn't believe it—
    no one moved,
    no one laughed.
    They sat there
        and they listened.
    I began to see kids wipe tears from their faces—
        there was a stillness,
            a quietness,
                a presence.
When I finished,
    I knew prayer wasn't allowed on campus,
        but we had gone that far,
            how could we stop?
    So I asked them to bow in prayer.

Afterwards they clustered around me,
        those who couldn't get to me
      reached out and touched me, sobbing
      "Thank you, Ann."
   "For the first time in my life, you've brought me
      hope."
      "Ann, I've never heard anything like that
      before."
      "Your God became mine today."
      "Ann, thank you."
I stumbled out of that auditorium
and across that campus—
      my back was a little straighter,
      my head tilted a little higher,

and the God inside me was a little bigger.
                I'm going where He goes ...
                    I am, anywhere
                And He'll be there beside me.
                The love for which He died ...
            not sophistication, or perfect words
                Is all I need to guide me.
                And He's my God ...
                    He really is,
                    Is He yours?
            And my silver brightly shining.
        He writes the music on a quiet summer morning.

                That's my story.

                I'm going where He goes—
                    out into the world
                    of lonely people.
            "Sir, can I take your hand?
                Or yours, ma'am?
                    Can I walk with you?
                        Can I laugh with you
                            and cry with you
                                and love you to Jesus?"

JOHN

You just can't stop love.
It crushes barriers.
It breaks and builds bridges.
It finds a way through.
It never gives up.
It's hard work.
It listens.
It walks ten extra miles.
It's something you do.
Jesus did it for me.
He died to set me free.
He lives to share my life with me
and I go to His
and my
people
and love wins.

One kid,
    his name was John,

walked around with his head down all the time.
He never looked you in the eye,
    and if you ever got close to him,
        he shuddered.
One day John wasn't there,
    and I said to the kids,
"Let's try an experiment.
    Let's really love John,
I mean,
    really love him.
As we've never loved anyone before.
    Let's just see what love can do for John."
He was the most inhibited, insecure kid
    I had ever seen in my life.
From that moment on
    we asked Jesus to help us love John.
Every time he came into a room,
    everyone wanted to sit by John.
We sent him letters.
    We wrote notes during the week.
    We stopped by to buy him a coke.
After six months of loving John
    the kids started to get tired.
    "Gee, Ann,
        you don't know what it's like to love John.
    You call him at home
        to see how his week is going
    and he says 'M-m-m, OK.'
        John, you say,

I really have been thinking of you
        and I love you
and he just grunts."

But I'll never forget the morning
    we were all gathered together
        and suddenly
                John smiled.
We had never seen John smile.
    He really smiled.
And two weeks later when he laughed out loud
    it nearly blew our minds.
        No one wanted John to notice
    but they were all trying to signal me—
        "Had I noticed?
            John laughed,
                he really laughed."

Three weeks later
    his mother, who was a non-Christian—
        the whole family was non-Christian—
    called me and said,
"Ann,
last weekend we were in the mountains camping.
    John is 16
and I haven't seen him cry since he was five.
    But he started to cry and bawl and sob.
And after four hours
    I was almost frantic

66

and I asked him why he was crying like this.
    All he could say over and over was
                        'I'm such a failure, Mom,
                        I'm such a flop.'
    And finally I said,
'It's that church you're going to,
    they're not treating you right.'
        And he said as he shook his head,
                'No, no.
                    It's my only hope, Mom.
                    They love me over there.' "
And she said,
    "It seemed like the minute he said that,
the minute he came out and shared that with me,
    he began to dry his tears,
and he straightened his back
    and held his head up.
And it's strange,
    he's never been the same since.

And in the group
    he began to laugh alot,
he began to share in conversational prayer when we
                prayed.
    He began to bring a friend on Sunday,
and two friends the next Sunday
    and he came the best softball player we ever had.
For the first time in his life
    he had the courage to play ball.

Love changed John's life,
just love.
You can do one of two things in your world.
You can build a wall
or you can build a bridge
to every person you meet.
I'm out to build bridges,
are you?
Come and build bridges with me.
Sir,
can I take your hand?
Or yours ma'am?
Can I pick you up little boy
and hold you in my lap
and kiss your cold face
even if it's dirty?
Can I love you to Him?
Can I love you so much
through thick and thin
until you learn
that Jesus really cares for you?
Can I love you until you feel hope for your world
and your tomorrows?
That's my hope.

That's my story
And it can be yours.

THE ARCHITECT

I started in Long Beach with 88 teen-agers.
I didn't know anything about being a youth director.
I just prayed one simple prayer,
    "Jesus, You called me.
    I am nothing
    but You are everything
    and I only make one request—
        that You do things
            so big
            so unusual
        that people will be able to look on
           with a sense of awe
           and say it is too wonderful—
        only God could have done it."

And then I didn't know where to begin
    but I told those 88 kids
        if they would just learn to love each other,

Jesus would trust us with the whole world.
                        But love is hard work
                    and it took a lot of months
        for the big, tough football players to learn to love
                            but they learned.
And in a year and a half
    we had Sunday School in three sessions on Sunday.
And we had Sunday School on Tuesday afternoons
    for the neighborhood guys who couldn't get in on
            Sunday,
            and three more sessions on Wednesdays,
            and a club on Thursdays.
                From Sunday to Sunday
                    in a year and a half
                we had four hundred teen-agers
                just because 88 kids learned to love
                    each other.

You tell me love doesn't work—
                    and I don't believe you.
Every time I went on a trip to speak
                those kids prayed for me—
                    twenty-four hours a day
                    around the clock—
because they were out to change the world.
    They'd say,
        "Ann, we can't fly with you
            but we'll stay here and pray."

An architect in our church walked up to me

and he was crying
and he said, "I want to tell you something.
A couple of weeks ago I got up early—
        at 4:30 A.M.—
            to fly to Panama
and I saw the light on under the door of my son's room.
            Now, Rick's a sharp kid
                but we can't get him up
                    even at 7:30 A.M.
            And here it was 4:30
            and the light was on in his room.
    I bounded across the hall and threw open the door
and I couldn't believe it—
there was Rick kneeling beside his bed with his Bible
            open—

                                    praying.

'Rick, what is the matter?
        It's only 4:30.
Are you having some special problem?'
                'It's Ann,' Rick said.
        'She's in Detroit this weekend
            and I pledged to pray every morning
                between four and five while she's gone.
        You know, Dad, we're out to change the world
            and when you change the world
                    you've got mountains.' "
                And the architect said,
    "I walked out of his room
    and closed the door
    and forgot my trip.

                        72

I went into my room
and fell on my knees by my bed
and buried my face in the sheets
and wept—
'Oh, Jesus,
I don't love you enough.
I don't care enough.' "

MIRACLE

I guess my faith for the world
   began when I was in Long Beach.
      I had read in the Bible about David and Paul
   and I began to pray,
      "Jesus, the world is so big and I am so small.
   Jesus, I want to see a miracle, too.
      Jesus, please bring a miracle into my life.
   I know you are big enough
      for my world today."

I was Director of Youth in Long Beach at the time
   and I presented it to my teen-agers.
      "Do you really want to change the world?
         Do you really want to?"
            And they did.
   We had learned to love each other
      and had a fellowship of several hundred in the
         group.

76

So I said,
    "Okay, let's begin to pray about a miracle.
I mean we read about them in the Bible all the time,
    but how many of you kids
        really believe that God is big enough
            to do what he did with twelve ordinary fisher-
                men today?"
        None of us seemed to really believe that.
    "All right, this is February.
This summer, let's take the first two weeks of July
    and during those two weeks
        we're going to pray together
            and laugh together
        and walk the streets together
            and share Christ together.
    And the last day of those two weeks is July 11th.
        I know this is just February,
    but somehow I believe that that should be our day.
        Starting now we'll begin praying for our
            miracle.
When you expect big things from God
    I believe He says, 'Are you ready?'
        July 11th is our miracle day."

You see faith is kind of like jumping out of an airplane
    from 15,000 feet up—
if God doesn't catch you—you splatter.
    But how do you know unless you jump?

February came and went.

March came and went.
    Whenever we had a big party planned
        the kids would say,
    "Ann, if we're expecting a miracle,
then maybe we should cancel the party,
    and go to the church to pray."
            So we didn't have one party in four months.
                I'd plan them
                    and the kids would cancel them,
                and every Friday night
            we would kneel around the altar of our church.
Under the great cross
    kids would pray simple prayers like,
    "God, I'm an ordinary kid,
        but I want to change the world.
        God, do a miracle for us,
            so we'll know You're big enough."
And we began to share with each other
    that with every miracle comes a sacrifice,
        that every great dream has its price,
        that this kind of dream is costly.

April came and left and the kids began to believe.
    My football players,
                big, tough ball players
    came to me and said,
"Ann, we just wanted to tell you
        that we got together and decided—
            well, we decided that, you know . . .

The coaches told us that if we weren't in practice
    the first two weeks in July,
            I mean those two weeks are really
                    important,
        that we couldn't play first string in the fall.
But we told the Lord
    that even if we couldn't play first string
            that the coaches would have to count us
                    out for those two weeks,
            because we were expecting a miracle.
    We're gonna try to change our world.
    We just wanted you to know
        that you could count on us."
I had parents come to me.
"Ann, don't you understand.
    We've been planning our vacation for a year.
And now John says he can't go,
    he's got to be here.
And those are the only two weeks."
            I said, "I don't know how to explain it to you.
                I feel inspired about it.
            We just want to know we serve a miracle
                    God.
                    And those two weeks are important!"
We prayed,
    we sacrificed,
        we believed,
            we began to give up.

I didn't know much about miracles

79

so I got my Bible and read about Esther.
She was a woman and so was I.
She wanted to save her nation
and so did I.
I didn't know much about miracles
so I read about hers.
It told about how she fasted for three days
before she went before the king.
I'd never really fasted much
but if she could, I could.
I told the kids that for the next three or four days
I'd be fasting
and if they wanted to join me
they could.

It was funny,
the second day I began to get phone calls.
"Ann.
How are you feeling?"
"Good."
"Pretty weak?"
"No, I'm feeling okay."
"Have you fainted yet?"
It was in June,
the day after I had ended my fast,
the phone rang in my office.
"Ann, this is so-and-so
I'm the campaign manager for
a well-known politician in California
who is running for Congress.
He's a Christian and I understand you are too,

and I understand you do a lot of speaking.
We need as much exposure for him as possible
and I was wondering if you could
            give him some of your appointments.
I'm sure you're interested
            in getting a Christian in Congress."
"Well, yes Ma'am.
    I certainly am.
        That sounds exciting.
    I'll see what I can do."
And just as we started to hang up, she said,
            "By the way,
                he is a very close friend of Pat Boone's.
            Now, I can't promise you anything
                by maybe, by chance,
            Pat could come to your city sometime.
                He's really very busy
                but maybe I could work with you and . . ."
"Thank you very much," I said,
    and hung up.
And the minute I put down the receiver it seemed to
            click.
    What if Pat Boone was to be our miracle?
        He could reach more people in one hour
            than we could find.
                    What if he came to our world?
    I ran into Dr. Gilliland, our pastor.
"I've got it!
    I've got an idea.
What if Pat Boone was our miracle?"

81

Stoic Dr. Gilliland looked up from his notes,
        "Do you know how much he charges?"
"Well, no, not really,
        I hadn't thought about it."
                "Try five to ten thousand dollars.
                I've already checked."
Five to ten thousand dollars,
        I couldn't even see the figures.
                All I had gathered was maybe two hundred.
                        And when I turned to leave, it clicked.
"That would be the miracle, Dr. Gilliland.
        He could come for free."
                        "Ann, would you please quit dreaming?"
I walked back
        and went through my speaking book
                and picked out some good appointments
                        and then did something that
                I didn't tell the kids about until weeks later.
I decided that there was no way I could touch Pat
                Boone
        unless it was through this politician.
I knew I'd have to see this congressman face to face.
        I'd have to share my story with him
                or he'd think I was crazy.
I called the campaign lady back.
"I have some real exciting appointments for you.
        But I've been thinking,
how can I support a man running for Congress
        if I don't even know him?"
                        "I don't know," she said.

82

"I just don't know if I could
         if I've never met the man.
So I couldn't give you my appointments
         unless I can meet him."
                  "Well now, he's a very busy man.
                        And I'm just a campaign worker,
                        I've hardly seen him myself."
"Well, I'm sorry.
         But that's the deal.
Either I get a personal appointment
         or I can't give up my speaking engagements."
         Well she was very huffy
                  and said that she'd have to see
                  and hung up.
                        I could hardly believe it
                  when she called back.
                        "I can hardly believe it
                              but he says he'll see you.
                        How about tomorrow about 11:00?"
"Great. Would you like to go with me?"
                        "Oh, I really would," she said.
"What is your address?
    I'll pick you up."
              I picked up the campaign worker I hardly knew
                        and headed for his office.
              I didn't know a thing I was going to say.
         There was only one thing I knew;
              a miracle is something only God can do.
And so I said,

"Jesus, if Pat Boone isn't to be our miracle,
        help me to really flub it."

And I walked into this plush office
        with all these impressive men standing around
                and he dismissed them and asked us to sit down.
And I don't know why but I just said,
        "Tell me why you are running for Congress?"
And he began his memorized speech about pornography
                and the poor legislation today
                        and he was just rolling along
                and right in the middle I interrupted him.
"Sir, do you believe in miracles?"
                        "Miracles?
                                Did you say 'miracles'?"

"Yes, sir.
    I'm asking you
because you haven't a chance
    of winning this election.
You have a very strong opponent.
        *I didn't have the slightest idea who his opponent
                was.*
                        He kinda laughed.
                                "I guess I better believe in miracles."
"Sir, I do.
    I believe in miracles,
but I never really saw one just for me.
    And I have some good speaking appointments lined
                up for you,
        but I have an idea.

84

I understand you're a good friend of Pat Boone's
    and Pat Boone could reach more people in my
        world in one hour
            than I could find in a year.
I know Pat Boone charges five to ten thousand
            dollars for any personal appearances.
And we couldn't pay him a cent."

By that time the little campaign lady was green.
    She wished she didn't even know me.
    She wished she hadn't come.
What kind of a fanatic was I?
    First, I asked him if he believed in miracles
        and then I asked if he could get Pat Boone
          for free.
        I got all ready for him to laugh.
          But he didn't.
He just casually pulled out his date book.
"Well, Pat and I are very good friends.
We keep each other's schedules,
and so I kind of know what his summer schedule is.
    Let me see here.
        Ann, I hate to tell you this
    but I see only one date all summer
        that Pat would be available
          and it's a Saturday
and you probably wouldn't want a Saturday
    but the only free day he has is July 11th.
July 10th he flies in from the Orient

and July 12th he takes his family to Europe
and well July 11th is it."

I didn't tell him that God had told me 6 months before
that July 11th was to be our miracle day.
I just looked up very solemnly and said,
"That would be a wonderful day.
Do you think it would be possible?"
He said,
"I'll see what I can do."
And I started out of his office.
"Ann, just a minute.
Ann, I'm a Christian but I'm a politician
and I almost forgot until today
that without God I am nothing.
Thank you for reminding me."
"Sir, you and I
both have miracles coming.
Could we pray together about them?"
And he cried and I cried
and we shared our Christ together.
And I walked out
and the little campaign lady staggered after us.
And I rolled down the windows of my Ghia
and headed down the freeway for home
and somehow in the deepest part of my heart
I knew a miracle was about to be born.
And I began to sing the two songs that were our
theme during that entire time.

Without Him I can do nothing.
Without Him I'd surely fail.
Without Him I'm just a drifting
Like a ship without a sail.

And with the wind blowing in my face
　　and laughing with the God of my life,
　　　　I began to sing.
　　　　　　　God can do anything.
　　　　　　　　　Anything,
　　　　　　　　　　anything.
　　　　　　God can do anything by faith.

I marched into Dr. Gilliland's office
　　and told him in no uncertain terms
　　　　he was about to see a miracle
　　　　　　and to just be ready for it.
I never mentioned Pat Boone to my teenagers
　　because I knew a miracle was something only God
　　　　　　　could do.
　　　So I wasn't sure that was to be it.
　　But my kids prayed
　　　　and we sacrificed
　　　　　　and the first week of July went by.
We laughed together
　　and cried together
　　　　and walked the hot streets together
　　　　　with perspiration dripping off our chins
We wore little cards with just two words on them.
　　"Ask me."

And we'd walk up and down the streets of our city.
"Excuse me, sir.
    See my tag?
Well, just ask me sir."
                        "Ask you what?"
"Ask me what the most exciting thing
    in my life is, sir?"
                   "What's the most exciting thing
                         in your life?"
"That Jesus is my friend.
    He laughs with me,
He cries with me
    and walks lonely roads with me."
        And on the street corners
           and in restaurants and parks,
    everywhere we went that week
        we shared Jesus, the Lord of our lives.
Monday of the second week came.
    I had not heard a word from anyone—
        the candidate or Pat Boone.
            And Saturday was our miracle day.
I had never mentioned Pat Boone to the kids.

And on Monday
    I felt led to write Pat Boone a letter.
I knew he got thousands of letters
    but I stuck a piece of paper in the typewriter,
        and typed something like this:
Dear Mr. Boone,
Hi! I'm Ann.

I believe in a big God and I thought maybe
you built your world around a big God, too.
You could reach more people in an hour
than I could find in a year. Could you
come for free? Just for an hour? To share
your Christ in my world?
If not, God has something better.

Good-bye King Boone,
Ann (Esther).

I sent it special delivery,
    I thought that might have a greater impact.
Monday went by
    and Tuesday went by
        and Wednesday night came.
    Everybody in our church was looking at me.
"Ann, I was young once.
    I dreamed big dreams once.
    But Ann, you can't put teenagers on the line like
        that.
        You shouldn't make them think
            that they can really change the world . . ."
On Wednesday night I said,
    "Jesus, this is my last act of faith.
        I'm going to call my brother."
You see, my brother has never been a Christian.
    Thirty-one years of age,
        he wasn't a Christian when he was five,
            he wasn't when he was 12 or 21,

he's never been a Christian.
He wears custom-made clothes
and buys custom furniture
and has an impressive job.
And I said,
"Jesus, I'm going to call my brother long distance
and tell him that I'm expecting a miracle.
And if there aren't any such things,
then there is no hope at all."
And I called him,
"Fred, my kids and I,
we're expecting a miracle
and Fred, you know what it might be?
I think Pat Boone's coming for free."
"Baby, if you want Pat Boone
I can get Pat Boone.
The Vice President of Paramount
is one of my friends
and Pat Boone would do anything for him.
I'll call him for you.
All I have to do is pick . . ."
"No, Fred, no.
Don't you understand?
A miracle is only something God can do."
"Well, I'm here to tell you Baby,
it'll never happen.
You'll never get Pat Boone for free."
And I hung up the phone
and I went to the window
and I shoved it up

and the cold air blew in my face
and I looked out at the thousand stars.
   "God, I've heard about miracles all my life
and I've read about them in the Bible,
   but God, I'm just an ordinary simple girl
and the world is so big.
God, how can I, a simple girl,
and a simple group of teenagers,
how can we change our world today
if you're not a big God for us.
God, no one seems to understand,
but I believe,
and I'm expecting a miracle."
"You know, Ann, it's Thursday
and the miracle is Saturday.
Do you think we ought to set up the sound equipment?"
   "What do we need sound equipment for?"
"Well, I don't know.
If it's going to be a miracle,
then it'll probably be pretty big
and we ought to get ready for it."
   "All right," I said, "I'll take care of it."
Another kid raised his hand.
"Ann, we've been praying and sacrificing
and giving everything we've got
for seven months
and day after tomorrow is the big day
and Ann,
have you heard anything?
Is anything in the air?"

"No, I haven't heard anything."
"Maybe we ought to go into the sanctuary
    and remind God we're expecting something."
                "Well," I said, "it's almost lunch.
                    What about lunch?"
He said, "I'll pray through lunch."
                "Allan, what about you?"
"I'm not hungry at all, Ann."
                "Jeannie?"
"I'm headed for the sanctuary."
                "Steve?"
"Who cares about food?"
                I said, "What if supper comes
                    and there's no reassurance?"
"We'll pray through supper."
                "And then what?"
"We'll pray all night if we have to.
    God's got to be a big God
or we don't have any hope. Ann.
    We're heading for the sanctuary."
            And they stood to their feet in silence
                with tears on their faces
                    and went to pray.

We hadn't been in the sanctuary more than five minutes
    when the secretary called me to the phone.
    I walked to the door and she said,
            "Ann, it's Pat Boone.
                He's on the phone."

92

"Oh, no," I said,
    "I never talked to a celebrity.
I'm not sure what to say."
        And I went down the hall
            and picked up the phone.
"Mr. Boone?
    Is this really you, Mr. Boone?"
            "Yes, it is, Ann.
                I just got your letter.
        I'm holding it in my hand.
                Ann,
                I never read a letter like yours.
                    I never knew a girl who
            has that kind of faith.
                    Ann,
                Shirley and I get in late tomorrow
                    and we fly to Europe Sunday,
                so Saturday, the 11th, is my only free day,
                    but if it will work for you,
                        we'll come on Saturday."
"Oh, Mr Boone, I don't know what to say.
    That would be wonderful."
                He said, "Would you mind
                    if Albie Pearson,
                the baseball player,
                    came with us?"
"That'd be great."
And I hung up the phone
        and for the first time in Ann Kiemel's life,
            I knew that it was no ordinary God

93

who walked with me.
It was a giant of a Lord,
and he and I—
we could change the world.
And I ran out and I said,
"He's coming! Pat Boone's coming!"
Every secretary in the office,
and Dr. Gilliland himself,
were running to keep up with me.
They were behind me in a steady stream,
as if I were the Pied Piper.
I ran into the sanctuary.
The kids knew nothing about Pat Boone
but I went bounding in and there they were—
all over the altars,
all over the platform,
crying.
I heard one kid just say this
"God, don't worry about me.
I'm believing."
I said, "Listen you guys,
it's happened.
Our miracle, it's happened!
He's coming.
Pat Boone is coming to us for free
Saturday morning at 10:00."
He can reach more people in our world in an hour
than we can find in a year."
And the kids stood to their feet

and we gave God the loudest, biggest standing
ovation
He's ever had.
And then, one by one,
my kids started getting down on
their knees
and one of the girls picked up her guitar
and with tears running in a steady stream
she began to play
and look up at the big cross
that we had prayed around for hours.
Without Him we can do nothing
Without Him we'd surely fail.
Without Him we'd be drifting,
  Like a ship without a sail.

But God can do anything,
        anything.
God can do anything by faith.

Saturday morning came
and needless to say everyone was excited.
All the newsmen had said
the deadlines for Saturday were past
but Pat Boone had never been to our city
and they were breaking the deadlines.
They had publicity everywhere,
they had it on TV,
they had it on radio,
they had it in the newspaper.

Saturday morning came and the place was packed.
>The aisles were lined.
>>There were people seated row by row in
>>the foyer
>and there were people seated inside the altars.
Church people?
>No, people from our world.
>>People who didn't know Jesus.
>Lost people,
>>hungry people,
>>>lonely people.
And Pat and Shirley whipped up in their little Rolls
>Royce
>and Albie Pearson crawled out of the back seat
>and we went into the office to pray
>and Pat and Shirley buried their faces and wept.
>>And Pat just kept saying,
>"Ann, show us how to find that kind of faith."
And Dr. Gilliland was saying,
>"We better go,
it's ten o'clock and they're waiting."
>>And Pat and Shirley didn't budge.
>>>"Ann, we want to change our
>>>world, too.
>>>How can we find
>>>that kind of faith?"
When we got to the platform
>it was my job to introduce Pat Boone.
>>And I walked to the platform
>>and I said,

96

"I am awed and moved today
   to be able to introduce to you
      my big God.
Pat Boone isn't our hero today,
   A big God is.
And that place,
   packed with hundreds and hundreds of people
      stood to their feet and cried and
         applauded
         and somehow God's spirit spread
            through
      and when it was all finished
         I calmly said,
            "And now I introduce to you,
               Mr. Pat Boone."
You ask those teenagers in Southern California
   if they believe in a big God.
      You ask them if they are afraid to dream big
         dreams,
         if they feel hope for their world.
      There is no question in their minds.
And people look at me and say,
   "Ann, do you?"
      "Yes, yes."
Though I walk through darkest valley
God, I know that to change my world
there are going to be some dark valleys,
but you've seen me through the dark valleys yesterday.
Though the sky be cold and gray.

Do you like cold, gray skies?
I don't
But there'll
be some for me tomorrow.
There's one for me today.
But God and I,
we've made it through the cold, gray skies yesterday.
We'll make it tomorrow.
Though I climb the steepest mountain
Do you know that dreams are made of mountains?
God, now that I've just conquered a mountain
do I have to climb another one?
Ann, don't you know?
Don't you know
that you've got to keep climbing mountains to
change your world?
But like a lamb who needs a shepherd by his side,
I'll always stay.
Give up?
Give up the dreams in my world?
Never.
Not ever.
God and I and love—
we're out to change the world.
God and I and love.

BLACK KNIT CAP

I had been at Long Beach two years
    when I got the call to be the Dean of Women at
    Eastern Nazarene College
I remember saying:

      "Uh-huh, Lord
      Dean of Women?
      I mean,
every dean of women I know is 70 years old.
And she wears her hair on her head in a bun.
    And Lord, I'm barely 26.
    I don't want to be dean of women.
      Boston?
    On the other side of the world?
    I don't know a soul in Boston.
I don't have one friend on the East Coast.
      Dean of Women?
    Give up 400 teen-agers

that I have laughed with
and cried with
and arm-wrestled with?
Leave them now?"
And I can still remember the few days before I left
When I told my teen-agers I was leaving
half of the boys
even the rough, tough football players
stayed home from school on Monday.
One mother said,
"John's in his room.
He's been crying all day.
He's never been like this before.
What should I do?"
I said,
"John's motto is 'Yes, Lord!' too.
He understands.
He'll make it."

And I can remember going to the gate to catch my
plane.
People thought I was some kind of celebrity
there were so many people there to see me off
I'm sure they were wondering.
They didn't know I was just ordinary Ann
except my teen-agers,
"Yes, Lord!" was their motto, too.

I can still remember as I walked through the gate
I heard a voice.

101

"Ann, Ann?"

When I turned around it was Jim.

Jim was a junior high boy
who had been won the year before.

He wore a little black cap.

It was his whole identity.

He took his little black cap off
and handed it to me over the gate.

"Ann,

hang this somewhere back there.

Put it on a peg someplace
so that when you're back there
and we're clear out here
you'll know God and I
are still changing our world."

And I tucked that little cap under my arm.

"Ann."

It was one of my high school boys.

He unzipped his jacket and pulled out a carving.

"Ann, take this with you, too.

It's pretty special to me,
but I wanted you to have it,
because I never want you to think for a minute
that because you're in the east
and we're in the west
that God and I'll stop dreaming.

If you're on the East Coast
and we're on the West Coast,
we ought to flip this world pretty fast."

And I was crying as I boarded the plane
    and the stewardess said,
"You must really hate to leave."
        And I looked at her.
        "I do.
            I love those kids down there, but . . ."
            I know where I'm going
            and I know who's going with me . . .

NEW NEIGHBORHOOD

I moved to Boston to a whole new world
  of big old houses on a neighborhood street
     and I was lost and frightened.
     An ordinary girl walking through a very big desert
     and a very big world.
     But I am a simple girl who doesn't walk alone—
     a great God has chosen to invade my life.

A girl who lived below me was a nurse
  and she found Christ.
     And there was another girl who lived next door.
     Her name was Barbara.
  I never told her I was a Christian.
    I just tried to love her
       and waited on Jesus to open the door.
  One day she knocked on my kitchen door and
    said,

                     "Ann."

She was crying.
   "Ann, just tell me one thing.
      You are always so happy.
         What is it that makes you so happy?"
"Well, Barbara,
   I've been wanting to tell you.
The most exciting thing in my life
   is that I chose to follow Jesus.
No one makes me,
   I chose to.
It was the most personal decision of my life
   and I have chosen to follow Him
because I know it pays.
   And because He loves me
and love makes all the difference."
                        "Ann,
                           how can I find Him?"
         And at the kitchen counter
            in my little apartment
               Barbara, my neighbor,
                  found Him.

A month later she moved out
   and another girl moved in
      and I couldn't wait for my first night home.
   I ran over and knocked on her back door.
"I just wondered.
   Do you go to church anywhere?"
         "No.
            I'm not exactly the church type."

"Oh, I see.
    I didn't mean to be offensive.
I understand
    but I have a very exciting church
and usually I'm out of town on Sundays
    but I was wondering
if some weekend
    when I'm in town
if you would want to go with me?"
                    "Well, I guess so."
The next week she knocked on my door.
    "Is this one of your weekends at home?
        I just want to go to church with you."
    And she did.
            But that wasn't when she found Christ.
        It was one night when I knocked on her door
            and sat at her kitchen table with her.
"Jesus Christ can make a difference in your life, Linda.
    He'll be your friend,
        He'll walk with you,
            He'll be your Lord,
                even as He is mine."
    And in tears at a kitchen table
        she accepted Him.

Two months ago she moved to Florida
        and now a couple lives in her apartment.
        I'm so excited.
    I'm out to love them to Jesus.
        And I will.

You watch,
    you wait,
        you'll see.
Give up?
Never.
    My aim is victory.
No matter how hard the road.
I have a giant of a God
    and He and I in love can do it.

THE SIDEWALK SWEEPER

A little old lady was sweeping the sidewalk
   and one day I drove up,
      and I was in a big hurry,
        and I looked up and said,
          "Isn't this the most splendid day?"
And she kind of looked up and nodded.
            "I have the most exciting God in me."
        And I ran on up the stairs
        and into my apartment
        and then it came to me
          that she lived next door.
     It was the wealthy little elderly lady
       that lived next door
         that was sweeping the sidewalk.
I had almost forgotten that she was part of my world.
           "Jesus—
        would You give me a chance
          to win her to You?"
It was about six months later

when I started to run into my apartment
and the little elderly lady stepped out.
                                    "Honey."
                    And I looked over and said
                        "Oh, how are you?"
She said,
"I've been watching you every day for a week.
I just returned from the hospital.
  I was lying on the bed dying
    and in my sub-conscious state
      I heard the doctor tell my family
        that I only had a few hours to live
        and I wouldn't make it through the night.
Lying there I thought of all the funerals I've ever
                    been to
        and I began to say,
        'Oh, God,
        if You will just help me
        talk to that girl next door before I die—
        there was something about her
        that makes me think she's got something
          I need.' "
And then she went on to say
    how the doctors couldn't believe
        that she lived through the night
    and how every day since she had come home
she'd been watching for me.

"How did you know about my God?" I asked.
"Do you remember the day

I was sweeping the walk
        and you told me you had
            a wonderful God inside you?
        There was something about the way you
            spoke—
I had never heard anything like that before,
        and I wanted your God, too."
"What is your name?"
                                "Mrs. Nelson."

"Mrs. Nelson,
would you like to go into your apartment?
It might be easier to pray there.
Would you like for my Christ to become your
    Christ, too?"
                And she began to weep
                    and we went into her elegant apartment
                and with her weeping and bent over
                    I began to share with her
                how my Christ could become her Christ.
                How He could laugh with her
                        and cry with her
                        and walk with her
                    even as He walked with me.

It was beautiful when I walked out of her apartment
        and realized I had changed my world in a little way
            because I had reminded an elderly lady—
                who lived next door in my world—
                    that Jesus lives and loves
                        and would walk with her.

JUNE

One day a girl came in on her bicycle.
She had another friend with her
    and this friend's father was president of the city
        college.
       And she was an agnostic.
         But I loved her anyway.
    I wrote poetry with her;
       I laughed with her.
    I arm-wrestled with her on the floor;
       I jogged with her;
    I rode a ten-speed with her.
I shared Jesus with her everytime I got a chance.

She would call me some nights
    and in the middle of a conversation
       she would slam the phone down in my ear.
    I don't know how often the phone slams in your ear
       but I didn't exactly appreciate it.

I mean after all,
    she was the one who called me.
But I loved her.
    Although, I really shouldn't say so
        because sometimes I really wanted to give up.
    And sometimes I really wanted to smack her in the
        mouth.
    But Jesus in me loved her.
          Through thick and thin.

And then one day seven months later
    the phone rang.
    She was sobbing and crying,
            "Ann,
        I don't know how to tell you.
          But today at school,
        in an unexpected, obscure moment,
            it came to me—
            God has to be.
Because no one in my life loved me the way you
        loved me.
If anybody can love me through my moods
          and the drugs
and all my mess the way you loved me,
       there has to be a God.
          Ann,
        in an obscure moment today
           I found him."
Just about a month ago,
    I got a letter from June.

She has Bible clubs everywhere.
Jesus is Lord of her life.
She's out to win her family to Jesus.
She believes.
Just because somebody loved her
through thick and thin
and you see, you can't stop love.
Love finds a way through.

BUSTER

A little boy knocked at my door one day.
    He was dirty and hot
        and he had wads of newspapers under his arm.
           "Would you like to buy a paper, lady?"
"Well, what kind of paper is it?"
              "Grit."

"Grit?
    What kind of paper is that?
I never heard of it."
           "Well, ma'am it's a paper I'm selling
             and it talks about . . ."

Well, I couldn't have cared less
    but I looked at him
        and he looked so tired and worn out
    so I said,
"Okay, how much?"
           "Quarter,"

So I went and got a quarter.
"What's your name?"
　　　　　"Buster."
"Hi, Buster.
　　My name is Ann.
Doesn't it get pretty hot
　　walking these streets every day?"
　　　　　　"Yeah."
"Pretty tired?"
　　　　　　"Yeah."
"Buster, I'd like to be your friend.
　　And whenever you're out selling papers,
if you get real thirsty
　　or real tired,
I want you to know you can come to my place,
　　and I'll give you some cold Kool-Aid
and let you sit down in the cool
　　and we'll laugh together.
How does that sound to you?"
　　　　　　"Pretty good."

And so Buster started stopping by my house.
　　I guess just because somebody cared about him.
　　　　And he needed someone to care.
One day I said,
　　"Buster, take me to your house.
I'd like to meet your family."
　　　　He sort of shuffled his feet.
　　　　　　"Gee, Ann.
　　　　　　　　It's not a very nice place

121

and I don't think you'd like it."
"Buster, I don't care where you live.
I just want to go with you."

He took me to a little shack with two rooms,
    a bathroom and one big room, and
        a father of some 80 years of age.
Buster, his little sister
        and his father all lived there.
Their alcoholic mother had deserted them years
                before
        and only dropped in now and then
            and the time I met her
        she had a big gash across her face
            where she had fallen.
I had never been in a place like that in my life.
    But I was out to love Buster to Jesus.
        He was part of my world
            and I really cared for him.
One day Buster said to me,
            "Do you like fishing?"
"Well, I guess so.
    I mean I'm not a very good fisherman.
I hardly ever go fishing."
            "Would you go fishing with me sometime?"
"Sure, I'll go fishing with you.
        Where do you go?"
            "Well, there a pretty good drain ditch
                up the road."
"Oh, when did you have in mind?"

"How about Saturday morning?"
"Saturday morning?"
    I had only one day to sleep in
            and that was Saturday morning.
                But, after all,
            if you love someone you have to make
                sacrifices.

"What time, Buster?"
                    "What do you say about 5:30?"
"Buster,
    I know the fish wouldn't bite at 5:30.
That's way too early."
                    "Yes.
                        That's the very best time—
                    5:30 in the morning.
                        That's when they really bite."
"Are you kidding me, Buster?
    Fish actually bite at 5:30 in the morning?"
                    "Sure they do."
"Well, okay love.
    Come by at 5:30
and we'll go to the drain ditch."
        If we were going to a big lake
            it would have been more exciting.
        But a drain ditch—
            at 5:30 in the morning?

He knocked on my door 15 minutes early
    and I wasn't out of bed yet.

I jumped into some old clothes
and we headed for the drain ditch.
He had dug a can of fat slimy worms.
When we got there I said,
"Buster, I tell you what.
I'll hold the worms while you fish
'cause I really don't know a lot about fishing.
You fish and I'll hold the worms
and maybe later we'll switch."
So I seated myself on a cold, hard rock,
holding the can of worms
and Buster went down to the ditch.
It was in his heart.
He wanted me to see him catch a fish.
He was determined—
And he tried.
He'd say,
"Shh."
"Buster, I told you it was too early."
"Shh.
Be very quiet."
So I'd sit there
looking at those ugly worms, praying,
"God,
Please help him to catch a fish
So we can hurry and go."
After a while,
the sky began to get darker and darker
and soon it began to pour.
"Buster, are you sure fish bite in the rain?"

124

"Sure, they bite anytime."
"Even in the rain, Buster?"
                "Yeah,
                        it's no problem."
And the water began to run in my hair.
    I was getting desperate.
"God, will you please hurry up?"
    Buster was not leaving without a fish.
            Finally he caught one.
    And we were both dirty
            and wet
                    and we got in the car.
            Now with a fish in the can of worms.
On the way home, I said,
    "Buster, are you hungry?"
                "Yeah."
"Would you like to stop at a coffee shop
    and get something to eat?"
                    "Wow! You mean a restaurant?"
"Yeah. Nothing special.
    Just a . . ."
            He thought he'd like that.

It just so happened
        that there must have been fifty businessmen
            having breakfast on Saturday morning.
                Well dressed, sophisticated.
            And we were dirty and smelled like fish.
        And they seated us and I whispered,
"Now, Buster you can have anything you like.

125

If you want five eggs
and three pieces of bacon
then you order it."
So he did.
I couldn't believe it.
Five eggs and bacon.
And when the waitress walked away he whispered,
"Ann, I never been in a place like this.
This must be the best in town!"
I couldn't believe that either.
But Buster had never been in a restaurant.
I loved Buster.
Everytime the social worker would come to his house
his father would send Buster on his bicycle
to me.
"Go get Ann.
I need her down here quick."
I made all the family decisions.
I decided what they did with their money.
I prayed them through the rough times.
I told the father what to do in every
situation.
He began to lean on me as if I were his eldest
child.
I baked fudge and cookies.
I'd laugh with Buster.
I'd walk with him.
Buster and I cried together.
Buster would tell me how embarrassed he was of his
house.

126

And every time I dropped him off
     my heart ached.
Did Buster come to Sunday School?
     Only about three times in two years.

But you see, I was out to love Buster.
     Not if he came to Sunday School.
          Not if he did what I thought he should.
     Just to love him.
          Through thick and thin.
     To love him even after I got him a new suit
     and he overslept
          and didn't make it to church—
     To love him anyway.

Buster's in the service now
     but I hear from him.
          He's about to get married.
     "Ann, there's only one person in my life
          who ever really loved me.
     And God lives in me because you loved me."
          Just a simple little thing like loving him
               brought God into the life of ordinary Buster.

A lot of times you tell people God is love.
                    And they laugh.
"Are you kidding me?
          Do you see where I live?
               Did you see my Dad beat me last night?

127

God is love?
I don't buy it."
The only love people in your world will understand is
you.
God and you loving them.
Then they'll believe.

MRS. GRISSOM

It was Saturday night
　　and I ran across the street to get the vacuum
　　　　　　　　　　　cleaner.
It was late
　　and I was tired
　　　　and in a hurry
　　and Mrs. Grissom handed me the vacuum cleaner
　　　　and I looked into her tired, old
　　　　　　　　　　　　　wrinkled face
and I don't know why
　　but as I took the cleaner and started to go
　　　　　　I said to her,
　　　　　　　　"Oh, Mrs. Grissom,
　　　　　　　　God loves you a lot."
And the tears just began to spill down her face
　　and she said,
　　　　　　"Could you wait just a minute?"
　　　　　　　　She went back into her house

and got a plaque off her wall
and brought it out.
It was a picture of weeds—
Just ugly old weeds smeared all over the picture
and underneath all those ugly weeds were these words:
Weeds
Nobody likes weeds.
Nobody carries them in a bouquet
or wears them in a corsage.
But God waters the weeds.
And she looked up,
"You know, Ann,
all my life
I have felt like a weed."
"Mrs. Grissom,
could I pray with you?
I didn't know anybody
went all through life
feeling like a weed.
There are times when I feel like a weed
but I didn't know anybody
felt like a weed all their life.
Really, I just came to get the vacuum cleaner—
but I was wondering
could we just stop for prayer?"

She said she'd like that
and we went into her little apartment
and I said,
"Would you like to hear

a little song
that I sing a lot in a big lonely world?"

**I will serve Thee
because I love Thee . . .
You have given life to me.**
*"So I'm not just a weed
and neither are you
because He gives us life."*
**Heartaches, broken pieces
ruined lives are why You died on Calv'ry.**
"That's why He came, Mrs. Grissom.
Your touch was what I longed for.
*"You see He makes flowers
out of weeds."*
You have given life to me.
And I prayed with her.
When I finished praying with her
I looked her in the eye,
"Oh, Mrs. Grissom
I love you.
You are
a very special lady to me."
And the tears
began spilling down her face.
"I've never been special
to anyone before."
I picked up the vacuum
and I ran across the street
to my little apartment

and threw myself across the bed,
"Oh God, it's so ironic!
The people who live closest to us
are the ones we overlook,
the ones we fail to reach out to.
Jesus, use me in the neighborhood.
If I am out to change the world,
I'll have to start in my neighborhood."
The next morning was Sunday
and I called the florist at 7:30
and asked him to put together
the most beautiful bouquet
he had ever fixed.
I wanted the flowers
that looked the prettiest
and smelled the best.
I mean the loveliest bouquet he had ever made!
"Well, look lady,
it's Sunday morning.
I barely have my houseslippers on and . . ."
"But sir, you don't understand.
It's for a very special lady
and I want her to know that she's not a weed—
but that she's beautiful."
"Yes, ma'am.
I'll see what I can do."
"Just write on the card—
'Bright Hope'—'Love, Ann.' "
The very next day
she knocked on my door

with tears running down her wrinkled face.
        "I never had a bouquet in my house before,
and Ann,
        for the first time in my life
I really knew God loved me."
I'm out to change the world—
        in love—
                that's my hope.

MARK AND ERIC, 5 AND 6

One day while I was sitting at my desk at ENC
    the housekeeper of Munro Hall called me.
"Ann, there are two little boys running in the halls
    and will you please come over
        and get them out?"
    You'd be amazed at the jobs a Dean of Women
            does.
        "I'll be right over."

I marched over and there were two little boys,
    their shirts hanging out,
        their hair in their eyes,
            their faces all dirty,
    running up and down the halls,
        slamming doors
            and banging on the walls.
I took them by either arm and told them,
    in no uncertain terms,

136

was I ever to see them in this building again.
In fact, in no uncertain terms,
    I was never to see them
in any building on this campus again
    or it would mean *"this."*
        I didn't tell them what *"this"* meant
            but by the look in their eyes
                I figured they understood.
Then I took each one by the hand
    and marched them over to my office
        and sat them down.
"Tell me your names."
                    "Mark and Eric."
"My name is Ann."
    "Oh."
"Can we be friends?"
    It seemed like a pretty good idea.
"Now that doesn't mean
    that if I catch you in these buildings
it will be less than *"this"*
    but I'll make a deal with you.
There's one building you can come to
    and that's this one
and only for one reason.
    That's to come and see me,
and you can come anytime you like.
    Is that a deal?"
            They nodded.
"And when you come,
    sometimes I'll buy you a Coke."

137

Now that really was a good deal
and out they went.

The next morning at 7:20
    I was running across campus
        and I heard someone calling,
            "Ann, Ann."
    And I looked over
        and there they stood.
            Mark and Eric.
"What are you doing here?
    It's only 7:20 and it's not time for school yet,
        is it?"
Their hands were buried in their pockets,
    sleep in their eyes,
        dirty faces and uncombed hair,
            and shirts hanging out.
    "But you said we could come anytime
        to see you."
"Have you guys had breakfast?"
    "No, our mom is a barmaid
        and she hasn't come home yet."
"Well, I've got to run
    or I'll be late for class."
    But I put my books down
        and my purse
            and knelt down on the sidewalk
            and put my arms around them both.
"I love you, Mark and Eric.
    Isn't it fun being friends?

Come this afternoon and we'll have ice cream."
　　　It turned out to be the first
　　　　　of many ice cream cones.

It was just about a month later.
　　I was in the bakery buying coffee cakes.
　　　　The kind you leave on porches of lonely people
　　　　　with little love notes on them.
　　It was a little love thought
　　　and I was late and in a hurry.
　　They were wrapping the boxes with string
　　　and I was writing a check
　　　　when out of the corner of my eye
I noticed a little boy
　　with a great big dog.
I really didn't pay much attention
　　but I heard the lady say to the little boy
　　　　"Do you want anything?"
　　"No."
　My coffee cakes were ready
　　　and I tore off the check,
　　　　　threw my purse over my shoulder,
　　　picked up my coffee cakes
　　　　and was headed out the door,
　　　when I stopped.
　　　　"Eric, I didn't know that was you.
　　　　　What are you doing at the bakery?
　　　　I know,
　　　　　I bet you wanted something to eat."
His hands were in his pocket

and his face was a mess, he shook his head,
          "No."
"Then I know, Eric,
          you just wanted to look in the window
                    because everything looks so good."
     And he said no again.
          I put my purse down
                    and lay the boxes on the floor.
I knelt by Eric and wrapped my arms around him.
          He kept his hands in his pockets
                    and his head down.
"Eric, you haven't been here all this time
          just to see me, have you?"
                    His head was down
                         but your could see this smile break across
                              his face
                         and he looked up out of the corner of
                              his eye
                         and nodded his head up and down.
"Oh, Eric, I love you."
                    And I kissed his dirty face.
"It's my treat today. Let's celebrate 'cause we're
                    friends.
          You can have anything you see."
                    "But I didn't want nothing, Ann.
                    I just came to see you."

I picked up my purse and cakes
          and headed out the door

with Eric behind me
        and a big dog behind him.

A little boy without a daddy,
whose mother works in a bar and is gone every night,
    a little boy that needed a friend
        and in my heart I whispered,
           "Oh, Jesus,
    help me to change his world, too."

CHOCOLATE CHIP COOKIES

Oh God, it's so ironic—it's so
ironic that the people living closest to us are
almost always the ones we overlook and fail to really
                    love—
I was out to love my neighbors to Jesus.
Everyday I would pray—
        "Jesus, what can I do
            to share you with them?"

It was a Saturday night
    and it had been several months of praying
        when I looked up into the cupboard
            and saw a package of chocolate chips.
    Now I'm not a special cook or anything
        but I can make pretty good toll house cookies,
            and I said to myself,
        "I'll bake them some toll house cookies."
And I threw everything together

and put the cookies in the oven
and when they were done
I threw them on a plate
and ran downstairs.
"Sir, hi.
My name is Ann.
And sir,
I baked some cookies for you and your wife.
I'm your neighbor from upstairs.
Well, I baked them for you, sir,
because I love you
and I—
well, what I mean is, sir,
I love you because Jesus loves me
and I don't know why,
He just makes me want to love you and your wife."

He looked blank
and shocked
and sort of helpless.
And suddenly I couldn't think of anything else to
say
and I felt foolish
and stupid
and sort of helpless, too.
And so I kind of shoved the cookies into his hand
and said goodnight
and tripped up the stairs
and ran in my apartment
and burst into tears.

145

"Oh, God, I blew it.
I really blew it.
What a ridiculous thing for a twenty-six-year-old girl
to do.
Take homemade cookies to the man downstairs
and tell him I love him.
He'll think I'm weird.
But God, you know what my motive was.
I was trying to tell him, Jesus,
that he is a part of my world
and his wife is
and I wanted to befriend them and love them to You.
Jesus,
can you make something out of this mess?
If you will, God, I promise—
I will never do anything irrational again.
I'll think it through clearly."

For three days I was heartsick.
I mean they didn't tell me they liked the cookies,
they didn't return the plate,
they didn't do anything.
But at the end of the third day
I was running up the stairs to my apartment
when there on the carpet
in front of my door
was an empty plate with a note taped to it.
I've never been so happy to see a plate in my life.
I ran in the door
dropped my books

and picked up the note
and began to read.

"Dear Ann—
Thanks a lot for the cookies.
We never heard anyone talk about God the way
you did.
I was in a convent studying to be a nun when
I met Mike
and we've wandered from God.
Could you come down
and have coffee with us sometime
and share your God with us?
Thanks a lot.
Mike and Kay."
I see people—
    warm faces,
        a running tear,
            a small child's hug,
                an old man's gnarled grip of love.
Saroyan said,
    "People is all there is—
        and all there was—
            and all there ever will be."

                    People—
                that's all that matters to me
                    that Jesus be Lord
                        and people.

147

IT PAYS

My brother who is 33 now
     accepted Christ two months ago.
        My brother, who laughed that God
          could bring Pat Boone to us.
     My brother,
        who had never been a Christian in his
         whole life.
I had written Pat Boone and said,
     "Would you look up my brother?
        Could you have lunch with him or
          something?
        Maybe you could reach him
         in a way no one else could."
        That was about three months ago.
And then about two months ago
   at three o'clock in the morning
     my proud, egotistical brother called me,
  "Ann, it's midnight here

and I know how late it is there
　　　　　but I want to tell you something.
I was down on my knees by my bed
　　and I got down with my face on the rug
　　　　and I asked the Lord
　　　　　　to give me somebody tonight.
Somebody to reassure me and tell me
that even after 33 years of sin
　　that God still loved me.
　　　　　　　And then the phone rang.
　　　　　And you know who it was, Baby?
　　　　　Pat Boone.
He said he had just tucked Shirley and the kids
　　in and he couldn't sleep
　　　　and he went downstairs
　　　　　　and he saw your letter
　　　that he had kind of forgotten about
　　and so he felt led to call me
　　　and tell me that God loved me
　　　　and he loved me
　　　　　　and could I come Tuesday
　　　　　　　to his house for Bible study.
Baby, let me tell you something;
　　God is love.
　　　　I know that now
　　　　　and you can count on me."

Ask my father if it paid for 33 years to walk the floor.
　　I used to hear him as a little girl, praying
　　　"Oh God, save my boy."

And today I'm 27 and my brother is 33.
When you hear my brother talk about the
Spirit and you hear him laugh
with the God of his life,
ask my father if it pays to hang on.
To believe in a faithful God.
To hang on.
What is your story?
The story of you.
How big are your dreams.
Your dreams for your world—
for your city.
**"By this shall all men know that you are my disciples
that you love one another."**
And with you and a giant of a God inside you
nothing—
nothing is impossible.
I like to sing **"Alleluia"** because **"Alleluia"** is praise.
Thank you Jesus,
thank you, Jesus, for being such a great Lord.
Thank you, Jesus, for love.
Thank you, Jesus, for hope.
You know what?
Love is hard work.
You know something else?
Love never gives up.
I wonder how many people are willing to say,
"Oh God,
I want more love today and tomorrow than I ever
had before.

152

Oh God,
I want greater faith.
I want to believe you're a bigger God
than I ever believed you were before.
God, I'm just one person,
but God you can count on me.
If you'll fill me,
and walk with me,
you can count on me, God."

I'M OUT
TO CHANGE
MY WORLD

Many of my weekends now are spent in traveling—
   speaking to churches
         and groups of men and women and boys
               and girls.
And every time I finish speaking I want to celebrate.
   I want to celebrate His love.
I want to celebrate the thousands of ordinary days
      when I thought I was not going to make it;
I want to celebrate the few big moments
      that have kept me going through the dark ones,
            and I want to celebrate hope.
Hope that there's going to be another side
      of this mountain or this desert,
            hope for the doors in my neighborhood
               that I haven't yet knocked upon.

Do you feel like celebrating?
A song I love to sing is "Alleluia."

156

Just that one word that means "Praise The Lord."
Alleluia for warm sun and blue sky
and a person next to me to call a friend.
Do you feel that way?
Let's celebrate together.
Do you know what my dream is?
That Catholics, Protestants, Jews can kneel side
by side
in backyards and churches
in living rooms and neighborhoods
and believe together that Jesus,
the Christ of our lives, can change our world.

And tonight in my hotel room I turned out the lights
and looked at the lights of a city
and wondered what kind of beautiful things Jesus
Christ could do if you and I joined hands
and let the Lord love through us.
And I prayed for every car that passed
and for every truck that was going up the freeway
ramp.
If Jesus could do so much through twelve ordinary men
what could He do through us?
And I wondered about Buster and June,
and the architect and Mrs. Grissom
and the taxi driver and a homeside G.I.
and about you
and I began to pray:
Oh, Jesus, Alleluia.
Thank you

for laughing with us
and crying with us
and walking us to the kingdom of love.
Fill us with your Spirit.
When we're scared give us courage
when we're weak make us strong
when we want to hate give us love and patience.
And may we wrap our arms around somebody
and love them to you.
May we cry with them as you cry with us,
and laugh with them as you laugh with us.
And may they know You by your love in us.
And that you and I and our brothers in love
can change the world.

BILLY GRAHAM

BOOKS TO BRING YOU COMFORT AND INNER PEACE.

____	80759	WORLD AFLAME	$1.75
____	80756	SECRET OF HAPPINESS	$1.75
____	80758	PEACE WITH GOD	$1.75
____	80757	MY ANSWER	$1.75

Available at bookstores everywhere,
or order direct from the publisher.

POETRY FOR
ONE AND ALL

	48820	IMMORTAL POEMS	2.25
	48785	POCKET BOOK OF	
		MODERN VERSE	1.95
	48753	RISING TIDES	1.95
	48808	ROBERT FROST	
		POEMS	1.95
	81319	POCKET BOOK OF	
		OGDEN NASH	1.95

Available at bookstores everywhere, or order direct from the publisher.